Praise for *The Five-Minute Medievalist*

"Laced with humour and written in a lively and engaging style, these delicious tidbits about the Middle Ages delight and inform, making clear the many connections between this earlier age and ours."

> Joanne Findon, author, *Lady, Hero, Saint: The Digby Play's Mary Magdalene*

"Danièle Cybulskie, through her frank, informative articles, reminds us that we moderns remain fascinated by the medieval. Cybulskie provides her reader with tidy, digestible summaries of medieval topics. To do so, she draws on contemporary scholarship which she then renders accessible to a wide audience. Her forays into the Middle Ages are guaranteed to spark deeper interest."

> Steven Bednarski, author, *A Poisoned Past: The Life and Times of Margarida de Portu, A Fourteenth-Century Accused Poisoner*

"The best kind of history will educate and entertain you. When you are reading Danièle Cybulskie's book, you will find that you've become a little bit smarter, and enjoyed the process. *The Five-Minute Medievalist* is a ... treasure for those who want to know more about the Middle Ages."

> Peter Konieczny, editor, *Medievalists.net*

The Five-Minute Medievalist

Copyright © Danièle Cybulskie (2016).

ISBN: 9780995151017

Cover Graphic: Eric Overton

Author Photo Credit: Daniel Cybulskie Photography
http://www.cybulskiephotography.com/

All rights reserved. No part of this publication may be reproduced, stored in a retrieval system, or transmitted, in any form or by any means, without the prior written permission of the author.

The author is not responsible for the content or persistence of external URLS, and does not guarantee their continued relevance or accuracy.

The Five-Minute Medievalist

Danièle Cybulskie

Preface

As a child, I was fascinated by the medieval fairy-tale world of King Arthur and Robin Hood, spurred on by my parents' love of Tennyson and Tolkien. It never occurred to me that this could be an area of study until I went to university and met some amazing professors who had, in fact, dedicated their lives to medieval literature and history. Once I realized that a person could legitimately spend all her time learning about the medieval world and its stories, I was hooked.

As I studied medieval literature in university, I realized more and more that the world is filled with misconceptions about the Middle Ages and the people who lived it. It became a minor obsession of mine to dispel these myths and untruths, and whenever I had some unfortunate person cornered, I'd pepper them with medieval trivia, such as the mind-blowing fact that medieval people never actually thought the world was flat. In 2008, I found myself a stay-at-home mother with a newborn, which limited my ability to shower people with medieval factoids. The bleary-eyed new mothers I met seemed to have more important things on their minds – like actual showers. With the encouragement of my social media-savvy husband, I took to the internet, starting *The Five-Minute Medievalist* blog with the idea of turning anyone into a medieval trivia expert in five minutes. Much to my shock and surprise, thousands of people around the world started to read it.

Although my love of the medieval never diminished, my dedication to the blog did. By 2010, I had two children, work at a college, and little time for anything else. Three years later, out of the blue, I was contacted by Peter Konieczny, who remembered my little blog. We met for coffee, and Peter asked to take on my old posts to see how they would fly with his readers at *Medievalists.net*. Soon enough, I was writing new articles weekly, then twice-weekly for *Medievalists.net* and had become The Five-Minute Medievalist.

This book is a collection of some of the most popular articles I've written from 2008 – 2016, and its wide variety of subject matter reveals the huge range of interests modern people have in the Middle Ages. Here, you'll find some popular myths busted, some answers to common questions, and some information that is as obscure as it is fascinating. With this book in hand, I hope you are inspired to keep learning more about the spectacular world of the Middle Ages.

Danièle Cybulskie
Toronto, 2016

A Note on the Text

This book started out as a series of articles on the web, then an ebook, both of which were peppered with hyperlinks instead of traditional references. In order to adapt it to its new printed form, I've used endnotes wherever the hyperlinks once were so that you can have a look at both my sources and the extra stuff I thought worth bringing to your attention. Although I've tried to smooth out the text to make these references seamless, you might still find endnotes in mysterious places. If you follow some of the URLs in the endnotes, you'll see just how deep the rabbit hole goes.

Contents

Ironing Out the Myth of the Flat Earth 1
Five Reasons We're Still Fascinated by the Templars 5
Medieval Parenting Advice 11
Five Great Ladies Who Refused to Be Quiet 15
The Tasty Medieval Pasty 19
Five Ways to Get Noticed by Historians 23
Medieval Myth-Busting at the Movies 27
Meet the Real Ulrich von Liechtenstien 31
Five (In)Famous Medieval Break-Ups 37
Five Fun Facts About Medieval Archery 43
The Medieval Sleeping Beauty 47
Five Surprising Rules for Medieval Monks 51
How to Tell if Your 12th-Century Lover is Just Not That into You 55
The Quirky Transformation of Five Everyday Words 59
Medieval Sex Lives: Five Frisky Facts 65
Acknowledgments 73
About the Author 75
Notes 77

Ironing Out the Myth of the Flat Earth

It seems there's one fact about the Middle Ages that always seems to astound people: medieval people did not actually think the world was flat. I remember being startled myself when this bombshell was dropped on me. If they didn't think it was flat, what did they think? And why are we all convinced otherwise?

Two big factors contribute to this oh-so-common misconception: a nineteenth-century author, and our own modern egos (although it has to be admitted that The Bible also muddies the waters). In 1828, Washington Irving wrote about medieval belief in a flat Earth in *The Life and Voyages of Christopher Columbus*,[1] which, while it sounds like an historical account of the titular life and voyages, was actually a novel. It must have been pretty convincing, given the enduring popularity of the myth of the flat Earth, but we shouldn't blame Irving entirely. The truth is, ever since the Middle Ages, society has been ready and willing to believe that our time is superior to the time that has come before. After all, we say to ourselves, medieval people didn't have smartphones. It's this superiority complex that has given rise to terms like "The Dark Ages" and "Renaissance" ("rebirth"); we, the modern people, feel free to judge whole historical periods and the people who lived them. While we certainly have superior technology in many respects, we should be careful not to assume ignorance in the people who came before us, since it can easily lead to our own.

You might ask, then, how it came to be discovered that the world was round. For this answer, we have to look up. In an age with no electric streetlights, people were constantly exposed to the brilliant beauty and predictability of the night sky. In order for the regular pattern of the stars to make any sense, either the Earth or the rest of the universe was moving around. An Arabic astronomer from the ninth century, Ahmad al-Farghani[2], supported this theory by pointing out that ships do not simply disappear from the horizon, as if they have fallen off: they slowly sink down until they cannot be seen. Al-Farghani was not the only one who noticed: the Earth is described as a sphere by the Venerable Bede[3] (seventh century), Roger Bacon[4] (thirteenth century), and Thomas Aquinas[5] (also thirteenth century), among others. Roger Bacon even guessed that the movement of heavenly bodies influenced physics on Earth. It wasn't only big thinkers that thought this way, either. The fact that the Earth's spherical shape was widely accepted is shown by the use of orbs as a symbolic part of royal regalia, and in pictures of Jesus, "The Saviour of the World" (*Salvator Mundi*).

Medieval astronomers didn't get the whole picture, though, since they believed that what was rotating around the spherical Earth was everything else. (Ironically, it was some of the revered Ancient Greeks that led them astray, notably Ptolemy[6].) The idea of an Earth-centered universe appealed enormously to the Christian church, which adopted it as truth. Theologically, it made sense that the centre of the universe contained Eden, and, more importantly, Jerusalem. Because the church backed this idea, it took great courage for later thinkers, such as Galileo, to challenge and change people's thinking, and the invention of the telescope helped to support the idea of a sun-centered galaxy.

A quick Google search will reveal how widespread the idea of a medieval flat Earth is, despite the flimsy evidence. Feel free to chase the myth as it pops up in everything from history textbooks to political speeches – just be careful not to fall off the edge of the Earth in your travels.

Five Reasons We're Still Fascinated by the Templars

If you've only ever dipped your toe into the medieval world, you've probably still heard about the Templars. Modern fiction's favourite bad guys, The Poor Fellow-Soldiers of Christ and of the Temple of Solomon (a.k.a. the Templars) was an order of military monks whose primary functions were in helping to "free" the Holy Land from Muslim control, as well as helping the pilgrims who traveled there. They were not the only such order, and never actually achieved their (later) objective to reconquer the Holy Land, yet a brief glance at the medieval history section of a bookstore will (more often than not) show more books on the Templars than any other subject. So, what is it about the Templars that makes them so fascinating?

1. They were impressive warriors ... and also monks.

Right away, the Templars seem to be founded upon a mystery: how can an order of monks be militaristic? Isn't that a contradiction? In a word: yes. However, the Templars were not the only Christians who believed that killing "infidels" was less egregious than allowing them to control the Holy Land. Plenty of popes were on board with the idea that there were different degrees of killing; for example, Innocent III forbade anyone to use crossbows on Christians, but using them on anyone else was not a problem. In fact, popes were behind many calls to crusade, so clearly, the contradiction between being Christian and being a soldier was not as big a deal to medieval minds as we might think. Still, the idea that those who devote their lives to being spiritually pure while also breaking one of the Ten Commandments is fraught with complexity, so wondering about the justification is a common draw, pulling the Templars into stories like that of Ridley Scott's *Kingdom of Heaven*[7].

2. They were also impressive bankers.

Being a part of a much-needed military unit in a conflict in which land is being conquered and parceled out is a recipe for becoming very rich very quickly. The Templars amassed a huge amount of wealth and land over the years; so much that they were able to lend out money to kings. Being great warriors with the integrity of monks, the Templars were also good people to store your money with. Because of their vast network and their capital, medieval people could deposit money at one temple and withdraw it at another. Like all bankers over the centuries, they were still sometimes vulnerable to robbery, though, with even Prince Edward (later Edward I, "Longshanks") of England succumbing to temptation, and robbing them of somewhere around a thousand pounds.[8] Anyone who controls that much money is rich pickings (pun intended) for villainy in medieval fiction, and the Templars unsurprisingly appear as a corporation in *Assassin's Creed*.[9]

3. Theirs was an order of secrets.

As members of a religious order, Templars were required to take vows, which understandably involved ritualistic elements, just as any other swearing-in ceremony would. The general public didn't seem to know much about these ceremonies, although there is some debate around whether or not the public could attend them.[10] Nevertheless, the fact that no one knew much about these rituals was turned around on the Templars when they fell out of favour, and their secrecy became the source of great speculation over what sordid deeds they were performing (more on that later). All of a sudden, they were "hiding" things from the people, and hiding, of course, never means anything good. Because few documents exists that outline Templar activities, their secret ceremonies are another great source for invention, as in Dan Brown's *The DaVinci Code*.[11]

4. They were present during the most famous crusade.

To think of crusading is to think of Richard I (the Lionheart) and his greatest foe Saladin (Ṣalāḥ ad-Dīn Yūsuf ibn Ayyūb)[12] who were at odds during what we now call the Third Crusade. The Templars were right in the thick of the siege of Acre, Richard's greatest victory in the Holy Land and also his greatest slaughter of captives.[13] To picture military monks there at the site of both Christian victory and the utter brutality of the crusades is to see them at their most powerful and most troubling. Given the moral complexity of crusading in general, the Templars' presence during this most famous crusade is good fodder for fiction. A novel which puts the Templars and Acre at front and centre is Andrew Latham's *The Holy Lance*.[14]

5. They had a famously brutal ending to the Order.

In the Middle Ages, money, politics, and religion almost always formed a messy and dangerous tangle. For the Templars, this culminated in the obliteration of their order, the torture of their members, and the fiery death of many, including their Grand Master, Jacques de Molay, in 1314. Their persecution was predominantly at the hands of Philip IV ("The Fair"), who arrested all the Templars in France at once, and proceeded to draw confessions out of them through torture. This arrest was unusual, since the charges against them were heavily religious (not civil) in nature, as a great article by Julien Théry-Astruc points out.[15] They were accused of heresy, including denying Christ and idol-worship, as well as participating in homosexual acts as part of their ceremony, although the evidence was scanty to say the least. Before the last executions were carried out, the Templars' reputation was dragged through the mud and has never really recovered. Because the Order was so brutally and thoroughly destroyed, and because the motivations behind their sudden destruction remain unclear, what the Templars' part in their fall from grace could have been is a compelling mystery. The curse of Jacques de Molay is the starting point of Maurice Druon's *The Iron King*.[16]

In a nutshell, the Templars remain compelling to modern minds because we just don't know enough about them to sate our curiosity. Everything about them is mysterious in some way, and the dark shadow cast over them by Philip the Fair remains to this day. No matter where you meet them, the Templars are a complex and interesting part of modern medieval fiction.

Medieval Parenting Advice

For as long as there have been children, there has been parental advice. Let's take five minutes to have a look at two Middle English texts that deal with advice: *How the Goode Wife Taught Hyr Doughter*[17] and *How the Goode Man Taught Hys Sone*[18] (both can be found in Eve Salisbury's excellent compilation *The Trials and Joys of Marriage*). Both of these texts were copied multiple times over more than a hundred years, which means that people thought they were worth the long labour of copying. So, what kind of advice would parents give to their children in the 14th and 15th centuries?

For both the daughter and the son, there is (first and last) an emphasis on observing religious duties, meant to help the children find both protection and comfort in faith. The children are encouraged to go to church and to pay their tithes so that they may be blessed. Bringing up faith both first and last is pretty common in many Western medieval texts, from stories to poems, and it sets the stage here for the type of behaviour expected.

In terms of good behaviour, the daughter and son are encouraged to be moderate, not hasty, and definitely not to laugh too loudly. The "Goode Man" says, "Lagh not to moche, for that ys waste" ("Laugh not too much, for that is waste"),[19] and the "Goode Wife" mentions laughing too loudly in the same breath as looking ugly, and behaving like a "gyglot",[20] which Salisbury translates here as "loose woman" (looking at the word, you can see its resemblance to our modern "gigolo"). The daughter is told to avoid gossip, and the son to be careful with his words. Both are also warned against the dangers of gambling and the tavern, and against wily members of the opposite sex: the daughter must not take "giftys" ("gifts")[21] from men who may be trying to seduce her, and the son must steer clear of "comyn women" ("common women")[22] because they will bring him nothing but trouble. This is pretty standard traditional advice, so is there anything moderns might find surprising in here? Maybe there is.

If you read the advice from the mother to the daughter, you come across many familiar themes, such as being a good housewife, keeping control of the servants, and not dressing too elaborately. Nearing the end of the text, however, comes a startlingly honest scenario:

And if it thus thee betyde,
That frendes falle thee fro on every syde,
And God fro thee thi child take,
They wreke one God do thou not take,
For thyselve it wyll undo.[23]

In other words, if you lose your friends and one of your children dies, blaming God will not help you cope. This stands out from the usual wise-but-distant advice, as it suggests that the death of a child would be such a blow to a woman that she might question her faith. I point this out because I think moderns cling to a couple of ideas about medieval people that are put to the test here: first, that they were somehow less attached to children (because they died so often), and second, that medieval people had an unshakable, unquestioned faith. That the mother in this text mentions this scenario as a possibility at all speaks to its likelihood, although this passage does not appear in all existing copies of the text (see Salisbury's notes). I'm guessing not all copyists wanted to contemplate (or perhaps think they were encouraging) the idea that faith could be shaken by the death of a child, but clearly the author and some of the other copyists thought this was as important to address as the other bits of advice.

What may be surprising in the father's advice to the son is that marrying a good woman who is poor is better than marrying a rich woman: that her possessions are not her true value as a wife. While the nobility had many arranged marriages in order to distribute or amass wealth, this advice suggests that money can't buy you love, and love is important to a good marriage. It would be going too far to say that this is a modern take on the spousal relationship, since the father admits that the wife is part "sirvunt" ("servant")[24] and part "fellowe" ("fellow" or peer).[25] Still, the father says explicitly "bete not thy wyfe" ("don't beat your wife")[26] because it will only make her hate you. Likewise, the son should not put her down, but treat her fairly. This is not the same as the "rule of thumb" type of relationship we often hear moderns assume that medieval people had.

While much of this advice is frozen in a cultural moment, there are bits of advice that will be completely familiar to us: go to bed early and get up early, be kind and generous, and remember that "many handes make lyght werke".[27] Like us, I'm sure that our ancestors took some of that advice and ignored other parts of it as they made their way through their lives. As readers, we can look at texts like these and find both good advice to live by, and an interesting portrait of the hopes of parents past.

Five Great Ladies Who Refused to Be Quiet

In the Middle Ages, the ideal woman was meant to be either a helpmeet in marriage, or a cloistered nun, obedience being paramount in both roles. Human nature being what it is, however, not every woman found it easy to fill one of those narrow roles in society. Although my list could be much, much longer, here are five great women who refused to sit down and be quiet.

1. Empress Matilda (1102 – 1167 CE)

Matilda, the daughter of England's Henry I, was the heiress to the throne, as well as Empress of Germany by marriage. Despite this, her cousin Stephen usurped her throne upon her father's death, but Matilda did not take this lying down. Unwilling to concede defeat, she gathered her forces and returned to England, deposing Stephen and taking back her inheritance. Unfortunately, the pith and vinegar that gave Matilda the impetus to march in and take over managed to alienate her allies within England itself, and soon enough Stephen was placed back on the throne. Although she was the rightful queen, she was never acknowledged as such, and is generally remembered as Empress Matilda instead of a queen of England.

2. Eleanor of Aquitaine (c.1122 – 1204 CE)

Eleanor is remembered as one of the most powerful women of the Middle Ages, and with good reason. She was Duchess of Aquitaine, Countess of Poitou, and Queen of France when she and Louis XII annulled their marriage over claims of consanguinity. Not long after the annulment, Eleanor married Henry II of England without bothering to ask for permission from Louis, likely because he would have refused the marriage: with Eleanor's land, Henry II owned more of modern France than Louis did. Passionate love may easily have been a part of Eleanor and Henry's courtship, and passionate dislike (if not outright hatred) was certainly a part of their long and tempestuous marriage. Refusing to be a quiet and obedient wife, Eleanor exerted a huge influence over her sons, encouraging their longing for more autonomy in ruling pieces of the kingdom. Henry was so convinced that she was behind the civil wars that erupted between himself and his sons that he kept her imprisoned (comfortably) far from court for many years. The rift between father and sons was never able to be healed, and Henry II died after submitting to Richard (I – the Lionheart) and John. Eleanor's hand in raising Richard was most likely the reason he was much more enamoured with Aquitaine than England itself, which he barely ever set foot in, as well as the reason the courtly love tradition began to flourish in England.

3. Isabella of France (1295 – 1358 CE)

Isabella was a princess of France, married to Edward II of England. Marriage to Edward was difficult for Isabella, however, as he was a weak king, in the habit of alienating the aristocracy by elevating his favourites (it's very likely these men were also his lovers) and showering them with outrageous gifts and status. Eventually, Isabella had had enough of Edward's ineffectual rule, and led an open rebellion against him, placing her son (Edward III) on the throne. Not only did she manage this through her vast influence, but she also held power enough that she was able to keep a lover, Roger Mortimer, without needing to keep the scandal too carefully under wraps. Eventually, Edward III separated them and executed Mortimer, but he never held his mother to the same account. Isabella's French influence was felt long after Edward's rule, as it was she (and through her, Edward III) who held a claim to the French throne, a major factor in The Hundred Years' War.

4. Joan of Arc (c.1412 – 1431 CE)

I mention Joan here because she was absolutely remarkable in her refusal to ever back down. A peasant girl from Domrémy, Joan managed to convince the local population, then high aristocrats, then the Dauphin himself that she was not a heretic, but rather a chosen vehicle for God's work. Rumour of her visions alone might have been enough to reignite the French army's low morale, but Joan actually put herself on the front lines of battle, again and again, despite this being absolutely contrary to all convention. Unfortunately for Joan, her obstinacy split the army between the path of her visions and the plan of experienced commanders, and she found herself excluded from strategy sessions and forays against the enemy. By the time she was captured by the English, her influence in France had waned, but Joan held to her convictions. She was treated badly by the English, and told she would escape burning if she would only confess to being a heretic. In a moment of weakness, she signed a confession, but the next day she took it back. Joan was duly burnt at the stake, only being canonized a saint many years later.

5. Christine de Pizan (1365 – c.1430 CE)

Christine was a contemporary of Joan of Arc, and she is said to be the first professional female writer. Widowed young with little children to care for, Christine used the education she had received at the insistence of her father to write poetry and prose for the French court. She wrote essays promoting peace, songs about her experience as a woman, and even a piece in praise of Joan. Most stunningly, however, Christine wrote *The Book of The City of Ladies*, a careful argument which takes apart all of the conventional arguments men made about women at the time. She wrote it in reaction to *The Romance of the Rose*, the content of which she strongly, vocally disagreed with. In *The City of Ladies*, Christine uses biblical stories, legends, and conventional wisdom to prove that women are smart, strong, loyal, and worthy of more respect than they get. Her careful logic and tact kept the book from being banned, and herself safe from prosecution throughout her long life. Unfortunately, *The City of Ladies* was not considered a vital part of historic study for centuries, which (in its own way) proves Christine's very point.

Although I don't have a book recommendation for Empress Matilda's life, I'd recommend Alison Weir's biographies of Eleanor of Aquitaine[28] (she also has written a novel on Eleanor[29]) and Isabella of France.[30] For Joan of Arc, check out Nancy Goldstone's *The Maid and the Queen: The Secret History of Joan of Arc*[31] for a look at both Joan and another influential great lady: Yolande of Aragon. As for Christine de Pisan, I highly recommend reading *The Book of the City of Ladies*[32] for yourself.

The Tasty Medieval Pasty

In keeping with the month's theme (July, 2014) of trying to make medieval stuff myself, I made an attempt at medieval cooking. What could be more medieval than a meat pie? In Hollywood and historical fiction, there always seems to be someone walking around a market square with a basket of hot pies, and I've always wanted to try one. It was definitely worth the effort.

The recipe I used is for "Lombard Chicken Pasties". It comes from *The Goodman of Paris* (which I've blogged about before [33]), and it appears in *The Medieval Cookbook* by Maggie Black.[34] This is a great book because Black has modernized all sorts of medieval recipes so that amounts and cooking times are all present, in addition to adding interesting commentary and background information. I'm sure that medieval cooks would have had a good enough idea of what to use and how much that writers didn't need to specify everything, but I am a modern girl, and I need specifics! While I definitely think Black's book is worth getting for her hard work and information, you can also find the original recipe from *The Goodman of Paris* and an alternative modern version at *Gode Cookery*[35] (an awesome website about medieval food).

To make Black's version, I first had to make puff pastry, so I relied on Gordon Ramsay[36] to show me the way. (Don't tell him that – because of a super-sensitivity to dairy – I had to substitute vegan margarine for butter!) Ramsay's recipe is easy and straightforward, and uses ingredients medieval people would have had access to: butter, salt, water, and flour. It does require that the pastry rest, though, so it takes a while to make.

(People without a dairy sensitivity can probably easily use a store-bought puff pastry dough, but I tend to err on the side of caution.)

After the puff pastry was made, the rest was pretty simple: dip some chicken (I precooked mine, just in case) in a mixture of egg and spices, place it on a pastry round, put a piece of bacon on top, brush the pastry with the egg mixture, fold it over, and crimp the edges. Pop the pasties in the oven, and you're done. Although The Goodman doesn't specify what spices to use, I used Black's suggestion of ginger and pepper. The only ingredient that isn't easy to get hold of is verjuice, but you can substitute lemon juice (Black's version) or wine vinegar (*Gode Cookery*'s version).

As I waited for my pasties to cook, I thought a little bit about this recipe in its time period. It's simple, and uses a minimum of ingredients, making it appealing to people who weren't terribly rich, and fairly easy to mass-produce and sell. It does involve two different kinds of meat, so poor peasants wouldn't have been able to eat it often, and no one (except rebels) would have been able to eat it on Fridays, or the many holy days on which meat was forbidden. It's the type of food that can be eaten hot or cold, which means it would be both a good seller in the market, and a good lunch to take to work. Being full of protein, a pasty would also be pretty nourishing all by itself. Altogether, a pretty great combination.

After taking the pasties out of the oven, I came to the moment of truth. I can honestly say the pasties were absolutely delicious! They were golden and crisp, with a great blend of meaty flavour inside. They didn't fall apart in my hands, didn't require any sauces to make them more interesting, and they were filling on their own. The pastry was rich, so it was good to have water on hand, but the flavours complemented each other nicely. Being a nerd, I wanted to see if they really were any good cold (as I imagined travelers and workers might have eaten them), so I saved some overnight, and they were just as good cold as they were hot. I will admit to not being able to taste the ginger and pepper, so it's likely the recipe is still good without those expensive (at the time) ingredients. (Also, you could avoid dealing with snakes...[37])

Although people will definitely look at you curiously if you tell them you're on a mission to create "medieval pasties", I'd definitely recommend trying these out for yourself. Making Lombard pasties is a fun and filling way to learn more about the past, and to share it with your friends.

Five Ways to Get Noticed by Historians

Of the millions of people who've lived on Earth, we know barely a fraction of their names. Even in periods in which thorough records were kept, time, the elements, and human actions have eroded our stockpile of documents, leaving us with just a few remembered names from the past. There are a few things that medieval people did that increased their odds of their names surviving, and they happen to be things moderns can do if they want to be remembered, too.

1. Get Arrested

Most of the ordinary medieval people whose names we now know have been discovered in official, legal documents. These could be ecclesiastical records (in which people were charged with fornication, adultery, and other sinful deeds), or manorial records (in which people made and resolved complaints about their neighbours' misdeeds), or court records (in which people appeared for big crimes, like murder). If a peasant committed a crime, it was recorded, and many of these records have survived due to where they were stored and who stored them. After all, government property is government property, and that tends to be respected except in cases of great social upheaval, like The French Revolution. Legal documents have revealed some fascinating medieval people, such as John/Eleanor Rykener,[38] a prostitute who worked dressed as both a man and as a woman. Without this arrest record, we would have no knowledge of Rykener; with it, we have both his/her name, and a very interesting case study.

2. Write a Memoir

It's true that most medieval peasants were illiterate, but that didn't stop Margery Kempe[39] from commissioning someone to write her biography. Kempe's story is one of marriage, pilgrimage, and the quest for greater spiritual understanding – it is also a record of one woman's attempts to be as saintly as she possibly could be, while annoying her neighbours ceaselessly. Anyone who has read *The Book of Margery Kempe*[40] will tell you that Kempe is unforgettable, and, doubtless, the medieval pilgrims who left her behind because of her incessant weeping would say so, too. Luckily, she has given us all a chance to remember her by having her story written down.

3. Graffiti

Medieval people sometimes got bored. Sometimes, they even got bored in church.[41] As a result, they wrote things on any available surface. Sometimes, they even left us a record of their names.[42] Because it's never smart for graffiti artists to leave enough information (time, date, address, etc.) for them to be tracked down, this is not as informative a method as the two above, but historians can make some pretty impressive inferences based on the script and the location of the graffiti. Either way, tagging a church or The Tower of London[43] will ensure that later generations are thinking about you as they sit where you once sat. (For medieval graffiti that goes beyond just tagging, check out Matthew

Champion's *Medieval Graffiti: The Lost Voices of England's Churches*.[44])

4. Make a Selfie

Imagine sitting and copying books all day, every day, knowing that your hard work is likely to go uncredited. Considering most copyists were monks, you'd think this wouldn't be an issue, but clearly some monks had trouble resisting the temptation to make themselves known, leaving their pictures and their names in the books they copied. The incomparable Erik Kwakkel has written extensively on medieval selfies,[45] and you can find his amazing pictures on his blog.[46]

5. Be Rich and Famous

This kind of goes without saying, but if you want to be remembered by history, you usually have to be rich and/or famous, or lucky. Since luck is something that can't be acquired (or maybe I just haven't yet learned the secret), being rich and famous works pretty well. We have plenty of information on the nobility of the Middle Ages because they left behind receipts, genealogies, proclamations, letters, literature, and art. Being rich and famous increased their luck in terms of being remembered, as there were more records left; even if some were destroyed, others would remain. If a person wasn't rich (like the Medicis[47]), she could be remembered by being – well, unforgettable, like Joan of Arc.[48] The more documents in which someone appeared, the more likely we are to have discovered them.

It's interesting to think of the possibilities future historians have for mining our own lives as we leave large, digital footprints every day. While we have a better chance of being remembered through channels that aren't illegal, it's fortunate that we have been able to find the number of medieval names and stories we have, largely through these five means.

Medieval Myth-Busting at the Movies

Call me masochistic, but I like to go see medieval movies at the cinema. I fully expect there to be a lot of historical inaccuracies, but what can I say? I like good, clean silliness as much as the next girl.

Thinking about the type of inaccuracy we often see in movies made me decide to do some myth-busting in this latest post. While I tackle some of the big myths (like Robin Hood[49]) in other posts, here are five of the most common myths about the Middle Ages, busted.

1. *Prima Nocta*

Speaking of movies, didn't it just make you so angry when you watched *Braveheart* and the evil King Longshanks (Edward I) and his nobles imposed *prima nocta* (that is, the right of the lord to sleep with any peasant woman on the first night of her marriage) on the poor, defenseless peasants? It was the catalyst for William Wallace's rebellion, and drove the whole plot of the movie. The thing is, *prima nocta* or *jus primae noctis* never existed, and part of the reason why is spelled out in *Braveheart*: the peasants were more numerous than the nobility, and the peasants would not have stood for such a thing. The other reason is that the idea went directly against pretty much all of the medieval church's teachings at a time when the church was a force to be reckoned with. This is not to say that nobility never stooped to rape, but it was not legal, nor was it acceptable. If you want to find out more about this enduring and widespread myth, Alain Boureau has written an entire book on the subject called *The Lord's First Night: The Myth of the Droit de Cuissage*.[50]

2. Medieval people had no table manners.

While food was eaten with hands, spoons, and knives (forks weren't popular in most of Europe until the seventeenth century), then, as now, eating was a communal activity, and since people most often shared plates and cups, it was not enjoyable if your companion had no manners. Entire treatises were written on correct etiquette, and encouraged things such as offering the best of the food on your plate to the lady, wiping your fingers on cloth, and wiping your mouth before taking a sip from your shared cup, so that you did not leave a slick of oil on top of the wine.

3. Open warfare was a daily occurrence, and consisted of two armies battling it out on a big field.

Warfare was very common in the Middle Ages (as in pretty much every other age), but medieval strategists were too sensible to frequently attempt the type of battle we often see in the movies. Having two big armies charge each other in the field was a little too risky – the outcome could go either way. Because of this, the most common type of warfare was siege warfare: an army would attack a stronghold, and their opponents would try to withstand the attack. For some entertaining views of siege tactics, check out *The Lord of the Rings* trilogy (you'll find sieges in *The Two Towers* and *The Return of the King*). While there weren't a lot of orcs and goblins running around medieval Europe, J.R.R. Tolkien was a medievalist, so some of the tactics are borrowed from history.

4. People used spices to cover up the taste of rotten food.

I suppose this might have been useful when there was very little food to be had (although, in that case, why would you have expensive spices hanging around?), but it was by no means the norm. Most people at this time were involved in agriculture – they knew when food was good and when it wasn't. There was little point in eating food that had gone bad, since it was risking making yourself dangerously sick, or worse. It is much more likely that spices, if used for camouflage, were used to make staple foods more interesting (much like ketchup).

5. Chastity belts

I saved this one for last because I know it may blow a couple of minds, but there is no evidence that chastity belts were ever made or used in the Middle Ages. Really. Someone made a joke once about chastity belts in the fifteenth century, but no one actually made a real one. That is, until the Victorian era, when people started to make "medieval" torture museums. To find out more about this ever-popular bit of misinformation, check out Albrecht Classen's *The Medieval Chastity Belt: A Myth-Making Process*.[51]

While I think this type of trivia is fascinating, you may find that it has either enhanced or detracted from your enjoyment of historical fiction. All I can hope for is that you find yourself feeling just that little bit more awesome the next time you watch a medieval movie.

Meet the Real Ulrich von Liechtenstien

If you've ever seen *A Knight's Tale*, you'll know that the titular knight takes on the name of Ulrich von Liechtenstein in order to joust on the tournament circuit and win the hand of his lady fair. What you may not have known is that there seems to have been a real thirteenth-century knight named Ulrich von Liechtenstein, who spent his youth jousting to win the heart (and body) of a capricious lady, and then wrote a book about it. Ulrich's book is simply called *The Service of Ladies*, and it is a fascinating tale of tournaments, ladies, and unrequited love - or maybe just lust.

According to Ulrich, he spent four years of his childhood as the page of a (never-named) married noblewoman. He learned as he grew that the greatest ambition for a knight was to serve a lady steadfastly and well, and to hope to be rewarded for such good service – preferably by becoming the lady's lover. Ulrich took this to heart, bringing his lady flowers, and even going so far as to secretly drink the water she used to wash her hands before eating. Eventually, he had to leave that household to learn how to become a knight, and he began tourneying in order to win himself (and his lady) honour in his late teens. He claims to have been one of two hundred and fifty knights to be knighted by Leopold of Austria at his daughter's wedding.

Realizing that his lady has no idea that Ulrich's tournament successes are dedicated to her, he decides to ask her to accept his service by using his aunt as a go-between, sending the lady a love song to please her. The lady accepts the song, and remembers Ulrich's service fondly, but refuses his love and service because of his "most unsightly lip".[52] In speaking to a friend, Ulrich mentions that his mouth "looks like three lips",[53] so it's possible he had a cleft palate or other long-standing physical difference. This is worth mentioning not only because it shows the shallowness of the lady, but because Ulrich opts for surgery to correct his lip, and then tells us about it. At first, his aunt and friends try to dissuade him – after all, any medieval surgery was potentially life-threatening – but Ulrich is determined, and finds himself a specialist in Graz who will operate. The doctor recommends that Ulrich be bound to keep him from moving, but Ulrich in his knightliness never moves "a fraction of an inch",[54] despite the surgeon's cutting. After a long recovery, Ulrich's mouth is declared "just fine"[55] by his aunt, but Ulrich's lady is only marginally impressed. She allows him to ride by her to speak his mind, but when he is too shy to speak, she tears out a lock of his hair while he lifts her down from the saddle as his just desserts. This is only one of the strange and violent episodes of this tale of chivalry. Another occurs when Ulrich severs a finger and sends a messenger to the lady for sympathy as it is slowly healing back onto his hand. She accuses his messenger of lying; after all, it doesn't count as severed if it's healing. As repentance, Ulrich re-severs the finger and sends it to her (she accepts it).

The central event of *The Service of Ladies* is an extended tour of southern Europe (referred to as the Journey of Venus) which Ulrich undertakes, dressed throughout in the guise of Queen Venus, in honour of love. On this tour, he gives out scores of gold rings, one for every knight who breaks a lance on him. He sends out advance notice to the cities he is going to visit, and knights come out in every city to win honour in the name of their own ladies against this knight in disguise. Although the description of the tour is much like Malory's *Morte D'Arthur* in that there are lots of splitting lances, lovely ladies appearing, and knights of unsurpassed chivalry, it's fun to poke through and see what might have been true in this sea of larger-than-life moments. One of my favourites is the countess who insists that Queen Venus lift her veil to receive the kiss of peace at mass: although she laughs when she recognizes him as a man, she kisses him anyway, on behalf of all womankind.

Despite all his efforts winning glory during his Journey of Venus (with a brief stopover to visit his actual wife), his lady is still unimpressed, and accuses him of being devoted to another woman (presumably not his wife). She then tests him again by making him stand outside her castle with the lepers, disguised as one himself, and leaving him to sleep out in the rain. The lady then decides to let him climb up a bedsheet to her chamber, but only to thank him for his loyalty: she has no intention of sleeping with him. When he insists that he's not going anywhere until she does sleep with him, the lady says she'll let him down the sheet and when he comes back up, she'll relent. The moment Ulrich is halfway down the sheet, however, she drops it. Ulrich is so distraught he just about drowns himself, but his messenger saves him with lies about the lady's promises. Trying to distract himself while he waits for the next rendezvous, Ulrich attends another tournament, at which point the lady tells his messenger that she'll sleep with Ulrich if he'll go on a sea voyage (the implication is of a crusade). He agrees, and she tells him that it's not necessary after all: she just wanted to see if he was loyal.

That summer, as he waits to finally be with the lady of his dreams, Ulrich says she does "an awful thing",[56] but he doesn't say what. He writes her a lament, and when she reads it, she does "a thing which hurt a lot".[57] After this unnamed thing, Ulrich finally gives up on serving his lady for good, and although he goes a while "lady-free",[58] he ends his book in praise of – and longing for – true love.

Ulrich's story tells us a lot about chivalry in that it shows there is a definite set of expectations placed on both the knight and the lady, not all of them healthy. For her part, the lady tells Ulrich over and over and over again in very explicit terms that she isn't interested in a relationship, and that she will never sleep with him, and yet he persists in the thinking that she owes him this in return for his good service. When she finally invites him to climb to her room, she has cleverly kept people around (including Ulrich's aunt) in the event that Ulrich may try to force himself on her. He admits that he'd "wrestle her", if those people weren't around, and that she would eventually "grant the prize of victory",[59] which tells you quite a lot about his romantic notions of the act. When she outsmarts him into climbing back out the window, it's not surprising that she drops him. One has to wonder what it could have been that finally made him give her up when being so blunt obviously didn't work. The fact that the narrative implies that she's being a tease and not saying what she means is a testament to the gender roles inherent in chivalry: both knight and lady have parts to play, and things don't end happily ever after when people deviate from the romantic ideal.

All that being said, it's impossible to know how much of Ulrich's story we can take seriously, especially because it so cleanly follows the narrative of knightly hardship in the name of a "coy" lady. Interspersed are vivid moments like Ulrich's surgery, the young boy drinking a washbowl of water, and the man huddled together with lepers and shivering in the rain. Taken as a whole, Ulrich's story is both a fascinating look at the self-invention of a medieval knight, and a tall tale all its own.

It seems fitting to end this short look at Ulrich's story with his own take on things, so I'll leave you with a short section from *The Service of Ladies*. Here's the lament that the lady found so offensive, called "The Twentieth Dance Tune" in this edition:

You noble ladies, so refined and lovely, take my part;
before you all do I accuse the mistress of my heart
for she has robbed me so of joy and left me only pain
that because of her I must   evermore complain.

I grieve that she'll not recognize my service, as is right,
although I've served her long and truly like a faithful knight.
That she is praised so highly everywhere by many a tongue
is because I've spread her fame   with the songs I've sung.

I charge my lady with committing theft and robbery,
for it is robbery and theft (what other could it be?)
that she should seize my happiness without declaring war
and deprive my heart of joys,   all for evermore.

I say she is a robber and is guilty of a theft

*so great I'll ne'er replace the things of which I am
   bereft.
If she should give me back enjoyment, which she can
   and may,
yet imagine what I've lost: many a lovely day.*

*Because of her I suffer more than I can tell or share
from agonizing, yearning pangs which secretly I
   bear.
Alas! Alas, that she was born to cause me such
   distress,
she whose love I most of all   wanted to possess.*

*Were I not silenced by manners and by hopes of
   love,
Then you'd believe, because of all the things she
   robbed me of
(should I reveal my longing heart and give each
   crime a name),
that the colour of her face   would turn red with
   shame.*

*If anyone can reconcile us this would please me so
I'd not be angry anymore nor burdened down with
   woe,
no one would hear me say of her a word of censure
   then
and, whate'er she later does,   this, at least, has
   been.*

Five (In)Famous Medieval Break-Ups

The other day, a friend put me on to the very funny *It Ended Badly: Thirteen of the Worst Break-Ups in History*[60] by Jennifer Wright, a modern and cheeky look at some truly awful splits from Emperor Nero to Debbie Reynolds and Eddie Fisher (and Elizabeth Taylor). Wright looks at two pretty nasty medieval break-ups, and I thought I'd expand on her idea a bit to include even more nasty break-ups, because – after all – who doesn't love a good train wreck as long as you're not on board? Without further ado, here are five infamous break-ups from the Middle Ages, starting with Wright's top picks.

1. Henry II and Eleanor of Aquitaine

Whatever these two were doing at any given time, you can bet that it was supercharged, from begetting heirs (they had eight children), to fighting. Wright chose Henry and Eleanor because when things went south for these two, they got medieval. Like, imprison-your-wife-in-a-tower medieval. Whether for political reasons – namely, Eleanor wanted to have more charge of her own hereditary lands – or because of Henry's longstanding mistress, Rosamund de Clifford (as Wright suspects), Eleanor urged her sons into open war against their father more than once, which landed her under house arrest for fifteen years. While Wright sees Henry's imprisoning Eleanor instead of killing her as partial proof of their love, it's more likely that Henry could never have seriously considered killing her, given that most of Europe – and his own sons – had too much respect for Eleanor for execution to have been an option. Although Henry was too smart to have destabilized his rule by killing his troublemaking wife, I have no doubt both of them wanted to strangle the other many times.

* *Bonus break-up*: Henry's infidelities caused more than one relationship issue, as he allegedly slept with his son Richard's (that's the Lionheart) fiancée, Alys, seriously straining relations between himself and Richard, as well as between himself and the king of France, her father.

2. Lucrezia Borgia and Giovanni Sforza

Wright's second choice for a bad medieval break-up is that of the marriage between two powerful Italian families that, well, were always out to get each other, which just goes to show that the whole woman-as-peaceweaver thing wasn't always a great idea. Lucrezia Borgia and Giovanni Sforza broke up shortly after their marriage in 1493, and her father (Pope Alexander VI) tried to persuade Giovanni to annul the marriage on the grounds of his impotence. Giovanni pointed to much evidence (namely illegitimate children) of this blatant untruth, and refused to lie. "And then," as Wright says, "the mudslinging started".[61] Giovanni spread rumours claiming Lucrezia was sleeping with her father *and* brothers, papacy notwithstanding; rumours so nasty and unshakable that they still haunt the Borgias' memory today. Finally, under intense pressure (i.e. death threats), Giovanni caved and agreed to lie. The trouble was, Lucrezia was now in the difficult position of having to swear to being a virgin while very, very pregnant. "The Borgia family," says Wright, "just decided to proceed as though she wasn't pregnant, and essentially dared anyone to bring it up. And it totally worked".[62] The marriage was annulled on the grounds that Giovanni was impotent and Lucrezia was a virgin. "There's nothing noble about this break-up," Wright concludes, "but it does seem like proof that if you do things with conviction you can get away with just about anything".[63] Just don't try this at home.

3. Pedro the Cruel and Blanche of Bourbon

In this break-up, the name of the man involved is kind of a spoiler in itself: no one gets a nickname like Pedro the Cruel by being nice to people. Pedro was a Castilian king, who loved his mistress and hated lots of other people. Being king, though, Pedro was obligated to marry someone suitable, so he was pressured into marrying sixteen-year-old French princess Blanche of Bourbon after dragging his feet for as long as possible. The two were wed with great pomp and ceremony, and enjoyed spectacular wedding celebrations for two days. On the third day, the groom promptly dumped his bride flat and returned to his mistress. Despite the horror and outrage this caused to the pope, the French, and the Castilians, Pedro never had much to do with his lawfully married wife after that, except possibly to kill her when she was twenty-five. As far as break-ups go, Pedro's was pretty darned cruel.

4. Peter Abelard and Heloise

So, this one may be a bit of a cheat because Abelard and Heloise didn't break up as much as they were split up by her relatives, but in terms of bad endings, their relationship deserves to be on every top five list. Heloise was a brilliant noblewoman who fell hard for her dashing tutor, the great thinker Peter Abelard, and the two began passionately sharing more than just intellectual ideas. Unsurprisingly, their secret love affair led to Heloise's pregnancy and the birth of their son, embarrassingly named Astrolabe. Abelard and Heloise married in secret, but their marriage vows were not enough to keep them safe from the wrath of her family: Heloise's uncle had men break into Abelard's room, where they castrated him. After his ordeal, both Abelard and Heloise joined monastic communities, quickly rising to the top by virtue of their brilliance. They never stopped writing love letters to each other, but their marital relationship in the conventional sense was definitely over.

5. Isabella of France and Edward II

Although Henry II and Eleanor of Aquitaine's marriage certainly contained more passion, Isabella and Edward II's had a much worse ending. Historians have long speculated that Edward II was possibly homosexual, which could explain his coldness towards his French wife, although she did bear him children. Nevertheless, it's very likely that Isabella outright hated her husband for his casual neglect, his foolish favouritism among his courtiers, or his disastrous ruling style – probably all three, and more besides. Like Eleanor, Isabella led her son into open war with his father, although this time, the people were on her side, and she conquered, placing her teenage son on his father's throne. The new Edward III, under the advice of his mother and her new lover (Roger Mortimer), had his father imprisoned, where he likely met his death. Whether Edward II was killed via a hot poker (which is extremely unlikely), by starvation (much more likely), or escaped to live out his life in hiding (as Ian Mortimer suggests[64]), his marriage to Isabella was an utter disaster by anyone's standards, and theirs was an unequivocally awful break-up.

For a great, fun read and more crazy historical break-ups, including Henry VIII and Anne Boleyn's, do check out Jennifer Wright's *It Ended Badly*. For more on Pedro the Cruel, check him out on Medievalists.net,[65] or read *Pedro the Cruel of Castile, 1350 - 1369* by Clara Estow.[66] For more on Abelard and Heloise, there's the great *New York Times* article "Heloise & Abelard: Love Hurts",[67] and for more on Isabella of France and Edward II, check out Alison Weir's *Isabella: She-Wolf of France, Queen of England.*[68]

Five Fun Facts About Medieval Archery

I recently spent some time learning all about medieval archery, and found some really interesting and odd facts to share with you. Here are five fun facts about medieval archery which you can use to impress your friends:

1. Medieval archers liked to wear decorative bracers.

As any archer will tell you, it's very handy to wear a bracer (or armguard) on the inside forearm of your bow arm for those times when your form starts to slip and the bowstring can whack you as you release. This is a very painful occurrence, and can leave a big, long-lasting bruise. Like modern archers, medieval people wore bracers, some of them very fancy indeed. Bracers could be made of leather (the most common), but also horn, silver, or even ivory, as Erik Roth notes in *With a Bended Bow: Archery in Medieval and Renaissance Europe*.[69] These could be carved or decorated to suit the taste of the archer, or of the lord he served.

2. Some feudal agreements required the service of a badly-equipped archer.

Feudalism was centered around the basic concept that people were permitted to own land under the condition that they owed military service in return. Feudal agreements spelled out each lord's obligation to the king, often in very specific terms, and sometimes these obligations seem a little strange. For some lords, land ownership was contingent on providing an archer to the king when he requested it, either for military duties, forestry duties (like hunting with or for the visiting king), or both. In some agreements, the archer in question was to appear when summoned without working equipment. As Richard Wadge notes in *Archery in Medieval England: Who Were the Bowmen of Crecy?*, the weirdest of these is in a record from the fourteenth century:

> *In 1342 Hugh de Grey was recorded as having held the manor of Waterhall in Buckinghamshire for the service 'of finding a man on a horse without a saddle ... a bow without a string and an arrow without a head in his army when the king shall order'.*[70]

This poor archer might have felt pretty nervous at the prospect of battle if he was ever summoned.

3. An increase in archery meant an increase in archery-related crime.

In the fourteenth and fifteenth centuries, as emphasis was placed on training soldiers to be proficient in using longbows for The Hundred Years' War, perhaps a predictable outcome was the increase in crime related to archery. As Wadge notes, bows and arrows seem to have been mostly used for premeditated crimes, as "a bow has to be strung first before it is used",[71] but an unstrung bow could also inflict some serious damage when wielded as a club. We also have records of bows and arrows being stolen, and of bows and arrows being used to apprehend criminals.[72] Everyone was being encouraged to have these weapons around and to know how to use them; it seems that they were definitely using them, for better and for worse.

4. Medieval archers often shot barefoot.

Medieval shoes didn't have the advantage of modern rubber grips; instead, most of them were leather soled. When archers shot a bow that was the same height as they were, with a draw weight in the neighbourhood of 100 lbs., it helped to have a little bit of grip to keep the bow and the arrow steady enough for an accurate shot. There's nothing quite like bare toes to keep you hanging on. (This factoid was brought to you by *Fighting Techniques of the Medieval World*.[73])

5. Medieval fire arrows were pretty impressive.

In his book, Roth gets into a pretty great discussion of fire arrows, which were used to devastating effect with some regularity. After all, many medieval structures and all medieval boats were made of wood, and therefore were extremely vulnerable to fire. Roth notes that European fire arrows had arrowheads in an s-shape (in cross-section) to better hold onto thatch, and used "pitch, resin, oil or naphtha on cotton or tow".[74] Apparently, the Muslim armies had even more impressive fire arrows which featured glass vials of naphtha at the tips that would ignite as they flew, allowing the arrows to explode in fire on contact.[75] These must have been terrifying weapons, and the fear of every sailor.

For more on medieval archery, you can check out my post on the longbow on Medievalists.net ("Why Was the Longbow So Effective?"),[76] and have a browse through the great books mentioned above.

The Medieval Sleeping Beauty

Compared to the friendly fairy tales of today, fairy tales of the past can often be – well, grim. One of the stories that spurred my interest in the Middle Ages as a child was Disney's *Sleeping Beauty*. Set in the fourteenth century, filled with colour and stylized images inspired by the Middle Ages, it's the classic story of a daring prince who battles evil to wake the sleeping princess with a romantic, chaste kiss. I've since read an early version of the Sleeping Beauty story from the actual fourteenth century, and it's much darker than the modern version, although it does hold an interesting secret for those who love the stories of the Round Table.

In the epically long medieval romance *Perceforest* lies the story of Zellandine, a beautiful princess from Zeeland who is in love with a knight named Troylus from Royalville, Scotland. One day, Troylus hears that Zellandine has strangely fallen asleep while spinning, and hasn't woken since. Troylus speeds to Zeeland to rescue her, and (after spending a week under a spell on a little side adventure) goes to the temple of three goddesses: "Venus, Lucina, goddess of childbirth, and ... Themis, goddess of destiny".[77] Troylus prays to Venus to discover how to wake Zellandine, and is told, "When you pluck from the slit / The fruit that holds the cure, / The girl will be healed".[78] If you've read medieval stories before, you probably know where this is going, but Troylus is oblivious enough to the goddess(es)' message that he is sent on his way with some impatience. When Troylus reaches the high tower where Zellandine is sleeping, a mysterious messenger appears who also tells Troylus to "follow the urgings of the goddess Venus"[79] and who magically transports him into the massively high tower, promising to come back at midnight. Troylus climbs in the window and finds the beautiful Zellandine sleeping naked (naturally) in a fantastic bed. He leans in to kiss her (asking her permission first), and is reminded by Reason and Discretion that "no man should breach a girl's privacy without her leave, and he certainly shouldn't touch her while she sleeps!"[80] Troylus hesitates, but then reminds himself of the healing power of kisses, and kisses her anyway. Zellandine does not wake up. Troylus, frustrated, rails against Venus for not telling him what to do, and Venus in her turn scolds Troylus for not getting her earlier hints: "You're all alone with this beautiful girl, the one you love above all others, and you don't lie with her!"[81] Troylus hesitates again, at which point Venus so inflames him that he does take Zellandine's "right to the name of maiden" while she sleeps, startling at a sound she makes and "ready to act all innocent"[82] if she discovers him. Zellandine still does not wake up, and just then the messenger reappears to hurry Troylus away before he is discovered. Quickly, Troylus exchanges back the rings that he and Zellandine had traded long ago (perhaps a belated attempt at making his misdeeds into a marriage) and follows the messenger, who has conveniently turned into a bird to carry Troylus away.

Nine months later, the still-sleeping Zellandine gives birth to a baby boy, who, in search of his mother's breast, suckles her finger instead. Zellandine immediately wakes up, and her aunt explains that, after Zellandine was born, she had made a feast for Venus, Lucina and Themis at the temple. Themis, outraged that she was not given a knife to eat with, cursed Zellandine so that

> *from the first thread of linen that she spins*
> *from her distaff a shard will pierce her finger*
> *and cast her into a sudden sleep, from which*
> *she'll never wake until it's sucked out.*[83]

Venus' plan has indeed woken Zellandine through a long and twisted route, although the aunt never does explain why she didn't bother to mention this curse earlier.

Eventually, Zellandine and Troylus run away together and marry, but Zellandine is shown to mourn her rape, even as she loves her husband. The baby, Benuic, stolen from the window by a half-woman-half-bird creature shortly after he wakes his mother, becomes a great knight, of course, and performs many great deeds.

In the *Perceforest* story lie the seeds of Sleeping Beauty as we know it: a supernatural woman angered at a perceived lapse in manners; a curse on a baby for its relatives' misdeeds; a finger pricked while spinning; a deep sleep; a high tower; a sexual encounter in sleep. Given the centuries between, this story is remarkably similar, although the modern version is very sanitized. And what is the mysterious connection to the Round Table? Troylus and Zellandine, through their son Benuic, are the ancestors of King Ban, the father of "the most illustrious man in all the world":[84] Sir Lancelot.

Five Surprising Rules for Medieval Monks

The Rule of Saint Benedict was one of the quintessential texts of the Middle Ages. It explicitly lays out how to effectively run and be a part of the ideal monastic community – at least in Benedict's view (there were many other types of monasteries, with their own separate rules). Benedict conscientiously records everything about everything, from eating and sleeping, to clothes, to the order of songs and prayers for services day and night. While the overwhelming focus of *The Rule* is on order and humble obedience so that everyone has a chance to attain perfection, there are a few rules which modern readers may find particularly interesting.

1. Age ain't nothin' but a number.

For Benedict, age is not nearly as important as wisdom or time spent in the monastic community. Throughout *The Rule*, he admonishes more senior monks to respect and care for their juniors, and he explicitly points out that "On no occasion whatsoever should age decide or predetermine rank, because Samuel and Daniel judged their elders as boys".[85] In fact, he also insists that junior monks be included in important decisions "because often the Lord reveals what is best to a junior brother".[86] "Junior" is a rank that could easily mean a more recently-joined monk, not necessarily a younger man, but Benedict insists that monks who are over fifteen should be accepted as full members of the community, and respected accordingly.

2. Novices were required to sign their lives away.

It's not a surprise that monks made a lifetime commitment to their monasteries, but it is interesting that Benedict insists that this commitment is made in writing. If a novice decides to stay on after his probationary year in the monastery, Benedict writes,

> *He should make a petition concerning this promise of his .... He should write it with his own hand, or, if he is unlettered, someone he asks should write it and the novice make his mark and place it on the altar with his own hand.*[87]

Like a secular contract, a novice's pledge of devotion was not binding unless it was signed, even if the novice could not read the words himself. Even boys who were given to the monastery were required to have a written petition from their guardians; the boy's petition was tied to his hand with an altar cloth when he was presented to the monastic community.[88] Both boys' and men's petitions were kept by the record-loving Benedictines long after they had been accepted into the community. Even if an errant monk is eventually thrown out, Benedict says, "he should not get back the petition that the abbot took from the altar, which should be kept by the monastery".[89]

3. Monastic crafts were great for bargain hunters.

As with many medieval Christian texts, *The Rule* has a very firm focus on humility. The section on artisan monks (Chapter 57) explicitly says that an artistic monk who becomes too prideful of his talent must "be banned from doing his craft"[90] until he has regained humility. The artist who is sufficiently humble, however, may have his work sold outside the monastery, although he must be sure that "the wickedness of greed should not creep into [his] pricing".[91] Benedict says that in order to not be too prideful, "goods should always be sold for a little less than can be done by others who are laypeople, 'so God may be glorified in all things'".[92] The handy upside of this is that it made monastic goods competitive, meaning that the monks could avoid being prideful while still generating business.

4. Strangers had to earn their kisses.

The Rule of Saint Benedict insists that travelers and strangers be welcomed as guests to the monastery "with every service of charity".[93] Monks are to meet them "with bowed head or the whole body prostrate on the ground"[94] as they would Christ, himself. Guests' hands and feet are to be washed by the abbot, and they are to have a place at the abbot's table at meal times. But, strangely, guests are still to be regarded with some suspicion – at first. When guests arrive and are greeted by the monks, Benedict says, "first they should pray together and thus be united in peace." But, he adds mysteriously, "This kiss of peace should not be offered until the prayer is finished, because of diabolical trickery".[95] While Benedict is very forthcoming in other sections of *The Rule*, he does not spell out what diabolical trickery monks should be guarding against. Perhaps, for a community with no real protection against violence within their walls, this communal prayer served as a sort of guarantee that their guests meant no harm.

5. Beware angry eyebrows.

Just as the thought of sin is enough to warrant penance, another monk's angry thought is enough to necessitate asking his forgiveness. Benedict requires his monks to be ever mindful of each other's feelings, "vying with each other for obedience".[96] Indeed, the ideal monk should be so very vigilant in his obedience that

> *if he even vaguely senses anger or distress, however minor, of any senior brother's soul toward him, he should at once, without delay, lie prostrate on the ground at his feet, making satisfaction until the disturbance is healed with a blessing.*[97]

(This reminds me of Maria von Trapp kissing the floor when she sees Sister Berthe coming, "just to save time".[98]) It seems to me that there might be a lot of prostrate monks at Matins if medieval morning faces were anything like modern ones.

The Rule of Saint Benedict provides a fascinating view into a large and influential section of medieval society through its theological viewpoint and consideration of daily practicalities. As such, it is definitely a worthwhile read for anyone interested in medieval life, monastic or otherwise. I highly recommend Bruce L. Venarde's translation for anyone new to *The Rule*, or for medievalists who love classy editions.

How to Tell if Your 12th-Century Lover is Just Not That into You

In the twelfth century, courtly love was all the rage with the French nobility. To participate in this trendiest of trends, though, you actually needed to know the rules. Enter Andreas Capellanus, author of *The Art of Courtly Love*, a book heavily based on Ovid, but with the definite thumbprint of its author. Although he is a *capellanus* ("chaplain"), Andreas is as interested in the ins and outs of love and sex as any editor at *Cosmopolitan*, and is full of scandalous tales (like that time he barely stopped himself from having sex with a beautiful nun) and helpful advice. There is so much about this book that is worthy of mention, but for today, here are five ways to know if your courtly lover is just not that into you anymore.

1. She avoids you.

Andreas says,

If you see that your loved one is missing all sorts of opportunities to meet you or is putting false obstacles in your path, you cannot hope long to enjoy her love.[99]

If she's missing your feast because she has to wash her hair, chances are she's just not that into you.

2. He asks for too many gifts.

When it comes to gifts, Andreas has many firm rules. It's okay to accept some (specific) gifts from your lover, but you should only accept money if you are in urgent need. Otherwise, you're not a true lover. Gifts, Andreas says, are a good test, because although someone who asks for gifts

> *may pretend that he is in love ... he is a long way from having the affection of a lover; what he wants is not to love, but to enjoy the wealth of somebody else.*[100]

Beware twelfth-century gold-diggers at all costs.

3. She spends too much time on personal grooming.

This is a tricky one, says Andreas, because she could be prettying herself up for you:

> *If you find that she is paying more attention to the care of her person than she had been doing, either her love for you is growing or she is interested in the love of someone else.*[101]

Don't jump to conclusions. If you want to find out for sure, just use "the greatest care and subtlety"[102] and pretend to be in love with someone else for a while. If she's jealous, you're good.

4. She tries to hide from your messenger.

This is the twelfth-century version of using call display, and it's a solid sign that your love affair is doomed, according to Andreas. He says,

> *if she tries to hide from your faithful messenger, there is no doubt that she has turned you adrift in the mighty waves and that her love for you is only feigned.*[103]

(Now you know how to answer you friends when they ask you about that girl who won't return your calls.) Andreas says that if she's not sending you messages, or if her messenger "is becoming a stranger to you",[104] it's pretty much over.

5. She's unenthusiastic in the bedroom.

Andreas doesn't shy away from talking about sex, but he uses the code word "solace" for propriety's sake (no one can accuse *him* of being smutty). When it comes to solace with your lady, pay close attention. For example, "if you find her, for no reason at all, growing half-hearted about giving you the usual solaces, you may see that her faith is wavering";[105] likewise, "if you find her less ready than usual to grant or to seek solaces, you may know that your love will not last much longer".[106] Ladies need good solace, too, so if she's not seeking solace with you, she may be seeking solace with somebody else. This may hurt to hear, but

> *if at the very moment of delight when she is offering you her sweet solaces the act is more wearisome to her than usual, or if you see that*

*your solaces bore her, you need not doubt that
she has no love for you.*[107]

Trust Andreas: the key to a good relationship is solace, so if the solace is boring, the relationship is probably already over.

When it comes to relationship advice, who better to trust than a twelfth-century churchman? For more helpful advice on love and solace, check out the rest of *The Art of Courtly Love*.

The Quirky Transformation of Five Everyday Words

The English language has undergone a whole lot of changes over two thousand years, from dropping letters (ash æ; eth ð; thorn þ; wyn ƿ; and yogh ȝ) to adding letters (w, z), to shifting its vowel sounds, to making the letters in some words silent (k, gh, e). Looking at a page from Chaucer or a page from *Beowulf*, it can be hard to believe that Modern English has any relation to the words of those long-ago authors. Although a lot of our words are recent additions to the language, thanks to Shakespeare ("excellent") and technology ("google"), the lion's share of our words stem from the Middle Ages. Here are five common words that we still use, but that have changed their meanings – sometimes drastically – over the last five hundred years.

check: "I'd better check to see if I have my dictionary."

This version of the word check comes through to us from the medieval game of chess, in which you still "check" people. Although its old meaning is a whole lot closer to "check yourself before you wreck yourself" – as in, stop yourself – it is the same word that gives us the meaning of being sure of something. Think about it: when you check your pockets for your keys, you've usually stopped moving. The first record of this word, according to the gurus at the *Oxford English Dictionary*, is in the late fourteenth-century, used by Chaucer to talk about two people being stopped in his poem *The House of Fame*: "They wer a-cheked bothe two" (l.2093).[108] Nowadays, check has expanded to mean both stop (as in to hold someone in check), and to check on.

This check is not to be confused with the check or cheque which you use to pay for something, since that has different roots. Check/cheque comes from "exchequer", the office of the English treasury, in which diligent accountants counted coins on a cloth made out of white and black squares, also giving us the words "checkered" and "checked". Medieval chess and checkers? Check and double-check.

gossip: "Have you heard the latest gossip about Chaucer and Gower?"

This is a word that only slightly bears a resemblance to its original meaning in Old English, which is basically "godparent" or relative through baptism[109] (J.R. Clark Hall simply defines it as "sponsor" in *A Concise Anglo-Saxon Dictionary*[110]). It comes from the words God and *sibb*, "relative", also the root of the more familiar "sibling", which comes to us unchanged from Old English.[111] The *OED* records the first instance of gossip in the context of a baptismal relation way back in 1014 CE, by Wulfstan in his *Sermo ad Anglos*. Because the people named as godparents are typically close friends or relations, by the time the word *gossib* showed up in William Langland's *Piers Plowman* in the fourteenth century, the word had evolved to mean "good friend" or "close friend". Who do you share all the juiciest news with? Probably your bestie. Over time, gossip changed its meaning from being the actual person you traded juicy information with to the information itself, or to someone who spreads it. While calling someone a gossip was once a positive thing that spoke to your relationship with someone, now it is a negative term applied to people with loose lips.

minion: "I'll just leave the cooking to my minions."

When I was a kid, a minion wasn't a yellow creature in overalls, but rather any willing stooge of a villain. Willing stooge is not too far removed from the way people used the word minion in the Middle Ages, depending on how much disdain was dripping from the word when they used it. Minion comes to English from French *mignon* and meant "darling", "favourite", and later "dainty"[112] (hence the darling little cut of steak, *filet mignon*). Those that a king kept close to him, were sometimes called *mignons*, being his circle of favourites,[113] and you can see how a term like that can easily devolve into mindless-followers-of-a-bad-guy, depending on how loved the king and his minions were. The word is first recorded around 1500 CE, and quickly changed meaning from just a favourite, to a favourite with negative or sexual undertones, most likely because sexual partners could hold a lot of sway over a monarch. Though the sexual implications seem to have dropped away completely, minion seems to have held on to its negative connotations; unless, of course, you're talking about a delicious cut of steak.

nice: "Medievalists are so nice."

Nice is a word which has made a complete reversal since the Middle Ages,[114] its odd flip in meaning even topping the list of "strangest changes" by *Oxford Dictionaries*.[115] That's because the little word we so often use to describe people we like literally meant stupid back in the day. Nice is from the Latin *nescius* – not knowing; *scire* is the Latin verb "to know", which gives us the words "science", "omniscient", and "prescient". The first recorded use of nice, as in stupid, is from around 1300 CE. In later centuries, people started to praise niceness – simplicity in a good way, it seems – and the term took a turn for the positive. For a medieval person, though, answering your spouse's "How do I look?" with "You look nice!" would definitely not have been nice.

silly: "What is with all these silly words?"

Silly is a word that I use pretty much every day – like most of us, to replace swearing – but it has nowhere near the same meaning as the word a medieval person would have used. Silly comes from *seely*, according to the *Oxford English Dictionary*, meaning blessed or happy. Its first recorded use is around 1450 CE in a story called *The Seven Sages*: "The sylyman lay and herde, And hys wyf answerd" (l. 1361).[116] For a modern person, to imagine a silly man and his wife does not conjure up images of goodness or blessedness, but more likely the tired stereotype of a man dangerously using power tools. Indeed, within a hundred years of this use, the term silly evolved into "someone deserving pity" and then "foolish", perhaps because the more cynical of us has always regarded the constantly-happy as being foolish, or at least blissfully unaware.

Bonus word!

undermine: "Jimmy is always undermining my efforts to become a knight."

Though the core meaning of this word is still basically the same, it's been separated from its medieval roots because people don't tend to literally undermine much anymore. The word actually describes a siege technique in which besiegers would dig – or mine – underneath the walls of a castle in order to collapse them. The first recorded use of this word is in the Wycliffite translation of The Bible, circa 1382 CE,[117] describing the way the walls of Babylon would be destroyed in the book of Jeremiah. While it's not likely that you'll be literally undermined anytime soon, next time someone tries to figuratively undermine you, remember there are plenty of siege tactics you can use to figuratively get medieval on them.

Medieval Sex Lives: Five Frisky Facts

So far, we've looked at chastity belts, sleeping maidens in towers, and dirty-minded chaplains – all the usual components of medieval sex, right? The truth is that, although the church did its utmost to ensure that sex was missionary-style and just for procreation, there was nothing that was going to stop medieval people from getting it on in all sorts of creative ways. Basically, if people are doing it today (and it doesn't involve batteries), people were doing it back then. That said, here are five frisky facts about medieval sex lives that you may not have known.

1. (S)expert witness testimony – it was a thing.

In the Middle Ages, both men and women were expected to have their conjugal needs met within the bond of matrimony, ostensibly so that they could have children. Not to fulfill the conjugal needs of your spouse was therefore grounds for annulment. Some records of annulment cases have survived, and they show an interesting twist: lawyers could call prostitutes to prove whether or not a man was impotent. At least one unfortunate soul has gone down in history for this affliction, the record showing that despite the prostitute's ministrations, there was not "any increase or decrease" for the poor man, aptly named John.[118] Another case, however, must have pleased the accused: the expert witnesses in that case proclaimed that the man was "large enough for any woman living in this world".[119] While prostitutes didn't get much respect outside of their work as witnesses, who better to call when you need a sexpert? Medieval people were nothing if not practical.

2. The men in gowns really did get down.

Like so many things, being celibate is easier said than done. Medieval priests were strongly discouraged from having wives and concubines, and we know this because the records show that priests frequently were in trouble for having common-law wives and concubines. Lusty priests were also a favourite subject of medieval jokes. One of my favourite thirteenth-century fabliaux tells the story of how God gave the care of harlots over to priests, and the care of entertainers to knights. The writer says of priests:

> *they're generous and serve their whores;*
> *their actions are my evidence.*
> *They lay out the inheritance*
> *and the wealth of Christ crucified,*
> *keeping their mistresses supplied*
> *out of their rents, tithes, and donations,*
> *and merit our congratulations*
> *above all others for this act.*[120]

The cheeky entertainer continues, "the clergy is assured salvation / and the knights will go to damnation".[121] Evidently, he was underpaid.

It was pretty tricky for clergymen to keep their affairs secret – their failing to do so is the subject of many a fabliau – and many times priests were in long-term, childbearing relationships with their mistresses, communities turning a blind eye unless there was a pressing need to make a complaint. Over the centuries, the church became more and more strict about this, but that didn't mean that priests stopped having sex. Beyond comfortable, steady, husband-like priests, there were also priests like Pope Alexander VI (a.k.a. Rodrigo Borgia), who – if snarky gossip is to be believed[122] – not only had children, but also had orgies with lots of prostitutes. And chestnuts. And prizes for sexual prowess. Clearly, the whole celibacy thing was considered by some priests to be more of a "guideline" than an actual rule.

3. Sex: it's good for you.

Medieval medicine was all about keeping things flowing, instead of letting them get bottled up. For this reason, orgasms were literally a matter of life and death. In a fourteenth-century French court case, a medical doctor testified that a man died of a heart attack, basically because his wife would not sleep with him.[123] Clearly, this kind of danger needed to be avoided at all costs, which is another reason why both men and women had conjugal rights within marriage. In fact, many medieval people believed that both the man and the woman had to experience pleasure in order to conceive. (Unfortunately, this theory has been used against women in rape cases up to, and including, the present day.) It was critical, then, that everyone should have lots of orgasms for their own sakes, and for the good of humanity. As with the Victorian health complaint of "hysteria", medieval women occasionally got sick from not orgasming, in which case they could be prescribed the treatment of manual stimulation by a healthcare professional.[124] Alternatively, they could choose another option…

4. Red leather sex toys: also a thing.

Not all sex is hetero or marital sex, and this was as true in medieval Europe as it is today. While sex toys are ancient, we know about their use in the Middle Ages mostly because of society's condemnation of any sexual activity that wasn't plain vanilla. For example, we know that some Italian merchants' wives turned to other women and sex toys to avoid getting pregnant while their husbands were travelling because a churchman groused about it.[125] Apparently, some nuns were tempted into sinning with sex toys, as well, since there is a stipulation in the *Penitential of Bede* which calls for seven years of penance for sex by "nuns with a nun by means of an instrument".[126] In 1477, court records indicate that the unfortunate Katherina Hetzeldorfer was drowned for living like a man with another woman, including having sex with her:

> *She made an instrument with a red piece of leather, at the front filled with cotton, and a wooden stick stuck into it, and made a hole through the wooden stick, put a string through, and tied it round.*[127]

Hetzeldorfer held the stick between her legs:[128] it seems to have been a medieval strap-on. Scholars tend to agree that much sexual activity between women flew under the radar because it didn't interfere with child-bearing; Ruth Mazo Karras notes there were only twelve such persecutions in the entire length of the Middle Ages (that we know of).[129] Hetzeldorfer's subversion of the "natural order" by living, dressing, and having sex like a man was too much for the court to ignore, though.

Because she played the man's role, her acts were considered much more egregious than those of her partners, and she was executed by being thrown into the Rhine. Her sexual partners were exiled.[130] The illicit nature and use of medieval sex toys (as well as the materials they were made of) means they were, and continue to be, very hard to find, but they do show an age-old connection between red leather and sex.

5. No pregnancy, no problem.

Many non-noble medieval couples did not get married until they reached their twenties, and it seems extremely unlikely that they all waited until they were married before having sex. Yet, records show that most women only gave birth to a few children, not dozens, especially if they were poor or lived in the city (for numbers and how to figure them out, see *Eve's Herbs: A History of Contraception and Abortion in the West*). The poor and the adulterous had a lot to lose by becoming pregnant, so it's not surprising that they did their best to avoid it. In fact, in the *Treasury of Medicines for the Poor*, a book meant to help the poor make their own remedies – authored, incidentally, by a doctor who would later become Pope John XXI[131] – one of the remedies is for "undesirable pregnancy"[132]: it's a contraceptive.

Contraceptive recipes can sometimes be a little tricky to track down because good Christians were not meant to prevent conception, but some of them have found their way to us. While some remedies were a little nutty – *The Trotula* recommends carrying weasel testicles in a goose skin around in your bosom[133] – others were herbal remedies that may just have worked. In the court case made famous by Emmanuel LeRoy Ladurie's

Montaillou,[134] a village woman testifies to having quite a lot of sex with a local priest (see #2 above), during which she always wore an herb on a string around her neck, which the priest placed "in the opening of [her] abdomen".[135] This could have been an amulet (as LeRoy Ladurie has suggested[136]), but I tend to agree with LeRoy Ladurie's second option – and John Riddle's guess – that it was a pessary, meant to disrupt the chemistry of the woman's vagina and prevent her from conceiving. Lusty priests were not the only ones who encouraged contraception, either. The revered physician Avicenna (Abū ʿAlī al-Ḥusayn ibn ʿAbd Allāh ibn Sīnā[137]) recommended women take (orally) "pomegranate pulp, willow leaves, colocynth, and pennyroyal"[138] to prevent conception if their health would be put at risk by pregnancy, and another author, Arnald of Villanova, even suggested that people might want to avoid pregnancy for non-medical reasons, including premarital sex. In his *Breviarum practice*, Villanova wrote a section entitled "Things so that a woman may not conceive in order that she might be seen marriageable".[139] It also includes willow leaves. As Riddle relates:

> *Some other recipes were grain, juniper seed, and ivy; the fern felix in a drink; elephant dung in a suppository; and frankincense, gum Arabic, myrrh and alum in a suppository.*[140]

Most of these ingredients would have been pretty expensive, but could easily have been worth the money for those women who wanted to remain in the marriage market and still have their fun. Chances are there were thousands of more affordable contraceptive recipes circulating via word of mouth and the town midwives that we will never know about. Because writing was the domain of (mainly religious) men, many of the sex secrets of medieval women will forever remain secret.

For more information on the endlessly fascinating topic of medieval sex lives, I highly recommend *Sexuality in Medieval Europe: Doing Unto Others* by Ruth Mazo Karras. John Riddle is the go-to man for information on medieval contraception and is the author of both *Eve's Herbs: A History of Contraception and Abortion in the West* and *Contraception and Abortion from the Ancient World to the Renaissance*. Finally, for some light-hearted stories that give you a sense of the medieval sense of humour surrounding sex, check out Nathaniel E. Dubin's *The Fabliaux*.

Acknowledgments

To have had any literary success, no matter how small, is to be indebted to teachers, and I was lucky enough to have had more than my share of amazing ones. I am thankful every day for the community of hardworking teachers who supported me throughout elementary and secondary school, and for the unending nurturing and support of my university professors, most notably Joanne Findon, Sarah Larratt Keefer, Fred B. Tromly and Alexandra Gillespie.

I am hugely indebted to the founders of *Medievalists.net*, Sandra Alvarez and Peter Konieczny, who have kept me supplied with free books and optimism. Their unending faith that I had something worthwhile to say has kept me going. Thanks for that coffee.

To the endlessly patient and loving friends and family who have walked beside me on the journey: there are no words for how much your support has meant to me. Thank-you from the bottom of my heart.

Thanks also to my small but mighty children for letting me fill your heads with stories of knights and castles, and for showing me your love by drawing trebuchets along with the rainbows in your pictures. Thank-you, especially, to my brilliant husband, who makes every day an adventure and everything a possibility.

Last, but not least, thank-you to my readers – both short-term and long-term – for inspiring and challenging me. It's been an absolute pleasure getting medieval with you.

About the Author

Danièle Cybulskie is a featured writer at *Medievalists.net*, and instructor for OntarioLearn. She studied English Literature and Cultural Studies at Trent University, and graduated with a Master's in English from the University of Toronto, where she focused on medieval literature and Renaissance drama. While she holds a special place in her heart for Middle English romances, her fascination with history extends to the minutiae of daily life for medieval people. Her mission is to share this love for the Middle Ages with modern people by making history fun and accessible, five minutes at a time.

Visit her website at www.danielecybulskie.com
Follow her on Twitter @5MinMedievalist
Rate this book on GoodReads.com

Notes

Ironing Out the Myth of the Flat Earth

[1] Irving, Washington. *The Life and Voyages of Christopher Columbus, Volume 1*. New York: G. & C. Carvill, 1828, p.77

[2] Abdukhalimov, Bahrom. "Ahmad Al-Farghani and his *Compendium of Astronomy.*" *Journal of Islamic Studies*. 10:2 (1999). 142-158. http://www.islamicmanuscripts.info/reference/articles/Abdukhalimov-1999-Farghani.pdf

[3] Bede. *On Genesis*. Translated by Calvin B. Kendall. Liverpool: Liverpool University Press, 2008, p.30.

[4] Cormack, Lesley B. "That before Columbus, Geographers and other educated people thought the Earth was flat." *Newton's Apple and Other Myths About Science*. Edited by Ronald L. Numbers and Kostas Kampourakis. Cambridge, MA: Harvard University Press. 2015.

[5] Weisheipl, James. A. "The Commentary of St. Thomas on the *De caelo* of Aristotle." *Thomas Aquinas: Contemporary Philisophical Perspectives*. Edited by Brian Davies. Oxford: Oxford University Press, 2002.

[6] DeWitt, Richard. *An Introduction to the History and Philosophy of Science*, 2nd ed. Chichester, UK: Blackwell Publishing, 2010, p.90.

Five Reasons We're Still Fascinated by the Templars

[7] "Kingdom of Heaven". *IMDB*. Last modified 2016. http://www.imdb.com/title/tt0320661/

[8] Morris, Marc. *A Great and Terrible King: Edward I and the Forging of Britain*. London: Windmill Books, 2009, p.56.

[9] *"Assassin's Creed"*. *Ubisoft*. Montreal, 2007. https://www.ubisoft.com/en-US/game/assassins-creed/

[10] Nicholson, Helen J. "How Secret was the Templar Admission Ceremony? Evidence from the Proceedings in the British Isles." *Medievalists.net*, February 27, 2015. http://www.medievalists.net/2015/02/27/secret-templar-admission-ceremony-evidence-proceedings-british-isles/

[11] Brown, Dan. *The DaVinci Code*. New York: Doubleday, 2003.

[12] "Why Does Saladin Have Such Good PR in the Medieval West?". *Medievalists.net*, September 1, 2014. http://www.medievalists.net/2014/09/01/saladin-good-pr-medieval-west/

[13] Deacon, Jacob. "How Far Were the Military Orders Responsible for the Results of the Third Crusade?" *Medievalists.net*, May 10, 2015. http://www.medievalists.net/2015/05/10/how-far-were-the-military-orders-responsible-for-the-results-of-the-third-crusade/

[14] Latham, Andrew. *The Holy Lance*. New York: Knox Robinson Publishing, 2015.

[15] Théry-Astruc, Julien. "A Heresy of State. Philip the Fair, the Trial of the 'Perfidious Templars', and the Pontificalization of the French Monarchy." *Journal of Medieval Religious Cultures*. 39:2 (2013). 117-148. https://www.academia.edu/4120353/_A_Heresy_of_State._Philip_the_Fair_the_Trial_of_the_Perfidious_Templars_and_the_Pontificalization_of_the_French_Monarchy_in_Journal_of_Medieval_Religious_Cultures_39_2_2013_p._117-148

[16] Druon, Maurice. *The Iron King*. New York: Harper, 2013.

Medieval Parenting Advice

[17] *How the Goode Wife Taught Hyr Doughter*. Salisbury, Eve, ed. *The Trials and Joys of Marriage*. Kalamazoo, MI: Medieval Institute Publications, 2002, pp.219-224.
[18] *How the Goode Man Taght Hys Sone*. Salisbury, Eve, ed. *The Trials and Joys of Marriage*. Kalamazoo, MI: Medieval Institute Publications, 2002, pp.219-224. pp.233-238.
[19] *Man*, l.67.
[20] *Wife*, l.49.
[21] *Wife*, l.91.
[22] *Man*, l.62.
[23] *Wife*, ll.171-175.
[24] *Man*, l.131.
[25] *Man*, l.132.
[26] *Man*, l.137.
[27] *Wife*, l.154.

Five Great Ladies Who Refused to Be Quiet

[28] Weir, Alison. *Eleanor of Aquitaine: By the Wrath of God, Queen of England*. London: Vintage, 2007.
[29] Weir, Alison. *Captive Queen: A Novel of Eleanor of Aquitaine*. New York: Random House, 2011.
[30] Weir, Alison. *Isabella: She-Wolf of France, Queen of England*. London: Pimlico, 2006.
[31] Goldstone, Nancy. *The Maid and the Queen: The Secret History of Joan of Arc*. New York: Viking, 2012.
[32] De Pizan, Christine. *The Book of the City of Ladies*. New York: Persea Books, 1998.

The Tasty Medieval Pasty

[33] Cybulskie, Danièle. "A Goodman's Guide to Marriage." *Medievalists.net*, June 14, 2014. http://www.medievalists.net/2014/06/04/goodmans-guide-marriage/

[34] Black, Maggie. *The Medieval Cookbook*. Los Angeles: Getty Publications, 2012, pp.46-47.
[35] Gode Cookery. "Chickens in Pastry in the Lombard Manner." Last modified 2000. http://www.godecookery.com/nboke/nboke18.htm
[36] Ramsay, Gordon. "Rough-Puff Pastry." BBC Good Foods. Last modified March, 2005. http://www.bbcgoodfood.com/recipes/2403/roughpuff-pastry-
[37] Cybulskie, Danièle. "The Wonderful *Wonders of the East*." *Medievalists.net*, May 22, 2014. http://www.medievalists.net/2014/05/22/wonderful-wonders-east/

Five Ways to Get Noticed by Historians

[38] "Top 10 Scandals of the Middle Ages." *Medievalists.net*, September 9, 2014. http://www.medievalists.net/2014/09/09/top-10-scandals-middle-ages/
[39] Cybulskie, Danièle. "Margery Kempe and the People on the Periphery." *Medievalists.net*, May 31, 2015. http://www.medievalists.net/2015/05/31/margery-kempe-and-the-people-on-the-periphery/
[40] Staley, Lynn, ed. *The Book of Margery Kempe*. Kalamazoo, MI: Medieval Institute Publications, 1996. http://d.lib.rochester.edu/teams/publication/staley-the-book-of-margery-kempe
[41] "Medieval Graffiti Reveals How Ordinary People Practised their Faith." *Medievalists.net,* July 11, 2011. http://www.medievalists.net/2011/07/11/medieval-graffiti-reveals-how-ordinary-people-practised-their-faith/
[42] "Medieval Graffiti Project Wins National Award." *Medievalists.net,* June 12, 2014. http://www.medievalists.net/2014/06/12/medieval-graffiti-project-wins-national-award/
[43] McQuillan, J. "The Subversive Pen: Prison Writing in the Tower of London." Mapping Shakespeare's London. Last modified 2011. http://map.shakespeare.kcl.ac.uk/blogs/map-articles/tower-of-london-forth-article/

[44] Champion, Matthew. *Medieval Graffiti: The Lost Voices of England's Churches*. London: Ebury Press, 2015.
[45] Kwakkel, Erik. "Medieval Selfies." *Medievalbooks* (blog), September 19, 2014. http://medievalbooks.nl/2014/09/19/medieval-selfies/
[46] Kwakkel, Erik. *Medievalbooks* (blog). Last modified February 16, 2016. http://medievalbooks.nl/
[47] "Tag Archives: Medici." *Medievalists.net*. Last modified August 29, 2015. http://www.medievalists.net/tag/medici/
[48] "Tag Archives: Joan of Arc." *Medievalists.net*. Last modified July 3, 2015. http://www.medievalists.net/tag/joan-of-arc/

Medieval Myth-Busting at the Movies

[49] Cybulskie, Danièle. "Robin Hood: The Original Rebel with a Cause and Fundraising Mascot." *Medievalists.net*, November 6, 2013. http://www.medievalists.net/2013/11/06/robin-hood-the-original-rebel-with-a-cause-and-fundraising-mascot/
[50] Boureau, Alain. *The Lord's First Night: The Myth of the Droit de Cuissage*. Translated by Lydia G. Cochrane. Chicago: University of Chicago Press, 1998.
[51] Classen, Albrecht. *The Medieval Chastity Belt: A Myth-Making Process*. London: Palgrave Macmillan, 2007.

Meet the Real Ulrich von Liechtenstein

[52] Von Liechtenstein, Ulrich. *The Services of Ladies*. Translated by J.W. Thomas. Rochester, NY: The Boydell Press, 2004, verse 80.
[53] Von Liechtenstein, verse 91.
[54] Von Liechtenstein, verse 95.
[55] Von Liechtenstein, verse 106.
[56] Von Liechtenstein, verse 1361.
[57] Von Liechtenstein, verse 1363.

[58] Von Liechtenstein, verse 1376.
[59] Von Liechtenstein, verse 1218.

Five (In)Famous Medieval Break-Ups

[60] Wright, Jennifer. *It Ended Badly: Thirteen of the Worst Break-Ups in History.* New York: Henry Holt and Company, 2015.
[61] Wright, p.53.
[62] Wright, p.54.
[63] Wright, p.55.
[64] Mortimer, Ian. *Medieval Intrigue.* New York: Bloomsbury Publishing, 2010.
[65] "The Most Dramatic Moment of the Middle Ages!" *Medievalists.net,* January 12, 2014. http://www.medievalists.net/2014/01/12/the-most-dramatic-moment-of-the-middle-ages/
[66] Estow, Clara. *Pedro the Cruel of Castile, 1350 - 1369.* Leiden, Netherlands: E.J. Brill, 1995.
[67] Nehring, Christina. "Heloise & Abelard: Love Hurts." *New York Times,* February 13, 2005. http://www.nytimes.com/2005/02/13/books/review/heloise-abelard-love-hurts.html?_r=2
[68] Weir, Alison. *Isabella: She-Wolf of France, Queen of England.* London: Pimlico, 2006.

Five Fun Facts About Medieval Archery

[69] Roth, Erik. *With a Bended Bow: Archery in Medieval and Renaissance Europe.* Dublin: The History Press Ireland, 2011. Kindle edition.
[70] Wadge, Richard. *Archery in Medieval England: Who Were the Bowmen of Crecy?* Dublin: The History Press Ireland, 2012. Kindle edition.
[71] Wadge, 2012.
[72] Wadge, 2012.

[73] Bennett, Matthew, Jim Bradbury, Kelly DeVries, Iain Dickie and Phyllis Jestice. *Fighting Techniques of the Medieval World, AD 500 - AD 1500: Equipment, Combat Skills, and Tactics.* New York: Thomas Dunne Books, 2006, p.153.

[74] Roth, 2012.

[75] Roth, 2012.

[76] Cybulskie, Danièle. "Why Was the Longbow So Effective?" *Medievalists.net*, October 18, 2015. http://www.medievalists.net/2015/10/18/why-was-the-longbow-so-effective/

The Medieval Sleeping Beauty

[77] Nigel Bryant, trans. *Perceforest: The Prehistory of King Arthur's Britain.* Cambridge, MA: D.S. Brewer, 2011, p.386.

[78] Bryant, p.389.

[79] Bryant, p.390.

[80] Bryant, p.391.

[81] Bryant, p.392.

[82] Bryant, p.392.

[83] Bryant, p.409.

[84] Bryant, p.412.

Five Surprising Rules for Medieval Monks

[85] Benedict of Nursia. *The Rule of Saint Benedict.* Translated by Bruce L. Venarde. Cambridge, MA: Harvard University Press, 2011, p.203.

[86] Benedict, p.29.

[87] Benedict, p.189.

[88] Benedict, p.193.

[89] Benedict, p.191.

[90] Benedict, p.185.

[91] Benedict, p.185.

[92] Benedict, p.185.

[93] Benedict, p.173.
[94] Benedict, p.173.
[95] Benedict, p.173.
[96] Benedict, p.227.
[97] Benedict, p.225.
[98] "The Sound of Music". *IMDB*. Last modified 2016. http://www.imdb.com/title/tt0059742/

How to Tell if Your 12th-Century Lover is Just Not That into You

[99] Capellanus, Andreas. *The Art of Courtly Love*. Translated by John Jay Parry. New York: Columbia University Press, 1969, p.157.
[100] Capellanus, p.159.
[101] Capellanus, p.158.
[102] Capellanus, p.158.
[103] Capellanus, p.157.
[104] Capellanus, p.158.
[105] Capellanus, p.157.
[106] Capellanus, p.157.
[107] Capellanus, p.158.

The Quirky Transformation of Five Everyday Words

[108] "check". *The Oxford English Dictionary Online*. Last modified 2016. http://www.oed.com/
[109] "gossip". *The Oxford English Dictionary Online*. Last modified 2016. http://www.oed.com/
[110] Clark-Hall, J.R. *A Concise Anglo-Saxon Dictionary*. Toronto: University of Toronto Press, 2004, p.158.
[111] Clark-Hall, p.304.
[112] "minion". *The Oxford English Dictionary Online*. Last modified 2016. http://www.oed.com/
[113] Allmand, Christopher. *War, Government and Power in Late Medieval France*. Liverpool, UK: Liverpool University Press, 2000.

[114] "nice". *The Oxford English Dictionary Online*. Last modified 2016. http://www.oed.com/
[115] Dent, Susie. "What Is the Strangest Change in A Word's Meaning?" Oxford Dictionaries, October 1, 2012. http://blog.oxforddictionaries.com/2012/10/change-in-word-meanings/
[116] "silly". *The Oxford English Dictionary Online*. Last modified 2016. http://www.oed.com/
[117] "undermine". *The Oxford English Dictionary Online*. Last modified 2016. http://www.oed.com/

Medieval Sex Lives: Five Frisky Facts

[118] Mazo Karras, Ruth. *Common Women: Prostitution and Sexuality in Medieval England*. New York: Oxford University Press, 1996, p.97.
[119] *Common*, p.97.
[120] Dubin, Nathaniel E. *The Fabliaux*. New York: Liveright Publishing, 2013, p.13.
[121] Dubin, p.13.
[122] Lee, Alexander. "Were the Borigas Really So Bad?" *History Today*, October 1, 2013. http://www.historytoday.com/alexander-lee/were-borgias-really-so-bad
[123] Bednarski, Steven. *A Poisoned Past: The Life and Times of Margarida de Portu, A Fourteenth-Century Accused Poisoner*. Toronto: University of Toronto Press, 2104, p.47.
[124] Mazo Karras, Ruth. *Sexuality in Medieval Europe: Doing unto Others*. New York: Routledge, 2005, p.112.
[125] *Sexuality*, p.112.
[126] *Sexuality*, p.110.
[127] Crawford, Katherine. *European Sexualities, 1400-1800*. Cambridge: Cambridge University Press, 2007, p.162.
[128] Clark, Ann. *Desire: A History of European Sexuality*. New York: Routledge, 2008, p.81.
[129] *Sexuality*, p.110.

[130] Clark, p.81.

[131] Riddle, John M. *Eve's Herbs: A History of Contraception and Abortion in the West.* Cambridge, MA: Harvard University Press, 1999, p.33.

[132] Console, Renzo and Christopher J. Duffin. "Petrus Hispanicus (circa 1215-1277) and 'The Treasury of the Poor'." *Pharmaceutical Historian*, 42:4 (2012), p. 85.

[133] Green, Monica H., trans. *The Trotula: An English Translation of the Medieval Compendium of Women's Medicine.* Philadelphia, PA: University of Pennsylvania Press, 2002, p.78.

[134] Le Roy Ladurie, Emmanuel. *Montaillou: The Promised Land of Error.* Translated by Barbara Bray. New York: George Braziller, 1978.

[135] *Eve's*, p.23.

[136] Le Roy Ladurie, p. 173.

[137] Flannery, Michael. "Avicenna." *Encyclopedia Britannica.* Last modified 2016. http://www.britannica.com/biography/Avicenna

[138] *Eve's*, p.103.

[139] Riddle, John M. *Contraception and Abortion from the Ancient World to the Renaissance.* Cambridge, MA: Harvard University Press, 1992, p.137.

[140] *Contraception*, p.138.

www.ingramcontent.com/pod-product-compliance
Lightning Source LLC
LaVergne TN
LVHW051604080426
835510LV00020B/3125